Radical Radiation!

Life in the Atomic Age

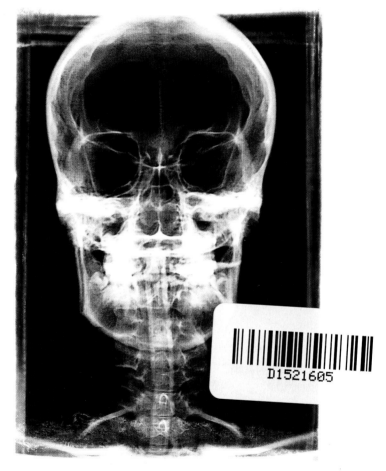

D1521605

P. Andrew Karam and Ben P. Stein

Steck Vaughn™

A Harcourt Achieve Imprint

www.Steck-Vaughn.com
1-800-531-5015

Radical Radiation! Life in the Atomic Age
By P. Andrew Karam and Ben P. Stein

Photo Acknowledgements
P. 4 ©CORBIS; p. 7 ©Bettman/CORBIS; p. 8 ©Michel Gendrault/
Roger Vernay; p. 15 ©Scott Camazine/Photo Researchers, Inc.;
p. 16 ©Martin Dohm/Photo Researchers, Inc.; p. 19 ©Bettman/
CORBIS; p. 21 ©CORBIS, p. 25 ©CORBIS; p. 26–27 ©Keystone/
Getty Images.

Additional photography by Digital Vision/Getty Images;
Photodisc Green/Getty Images.

ISBN 1-4190-2278-4

Printed in China
4 5 6 7 8 788 12 11 10 09 08 07

Table of Contents

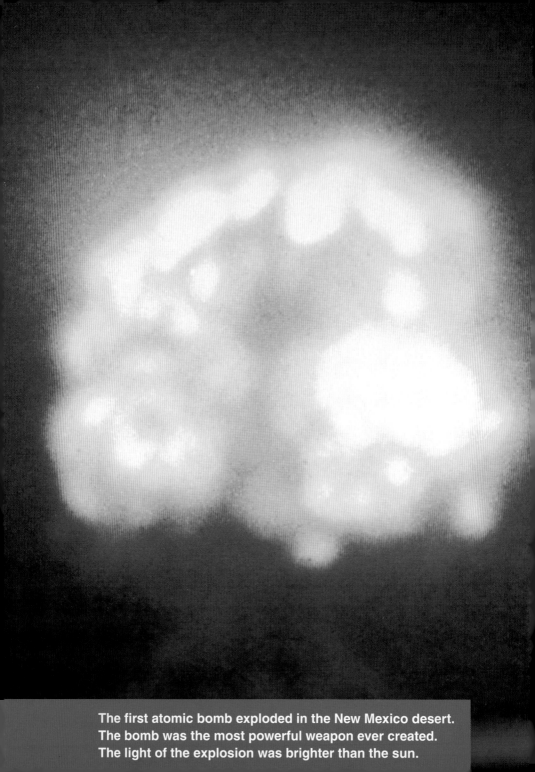

The first atomic bomb exploded in the New Mexico desert.
The bomb was the most powerful weapon ever created.
The light of the explosion was brighter than the sun.

Introduction
The Power of the Atom

On July 16, 1945, a group of scientists waited in the New Mexico desert. It was still dark. Six miles away stood a five-foot metal ball. This was the world's first atomic bomb.

Would it work? No one knew.

Then, at 5:30 A.M., a blinding light lit the desert. A wave of heat spread through the cool dawn. The scientists turned to look. A huge mushroom-shaped cloud rose to the sky. The world's most powerful bomb had exploded.

Where did the bomb get its power? It came from one of the smallest things on Earth: the **atom**. Everything in the world is made of atoms. Atoms are unbelievably tiny. How small? Place a million of them in a line. That line would fit inside the period at the end of this sentence.

Inside the tiny atom lies tremendous power. In the last 100 years, we've learned to use that power. It has changed our world. We use atomic power to make electricity. That same power also lets us look inside the human body. It helps us treat cancer. How is this possible? Let's find out.

CHAPTER 1

Discovery!

For many thousands of years, humans lived without electricity. Their light came from sunlight or fire. Animals helped with hard work and travel.

Then, new types of machines began the age of technology. In the late 1800s, cars were invented. Americans started to use telephones. Cities were lit with electric lights. Scientists learned more about the **elements** that make up our world. The secret of the atom would soon be uncovered.

It was November of 1895. German scientist Wilhelm Roentgen was puzzled. He was working with a cathode ray tube. Inside this device, a ray of electricity traveled between two pieces of metal. Roentgen noticed something strange. He had covered the tube with black paper. Yet across the room, a metal-coated screen was glowing. He put a thick book in front of the screen. The screen still glowed. Somehow, the cathode ray tube was causing this. Some kind of ray was escaping from the tube.

The ray couldn't be electricity. Electricity needs a conductor, like a metal wire or even water. Electricity couldn't travel that far through the air unnoticed.

Roentgen didn't know what caused the metal screen to glow. He wasn't sure how the ray passed through solid objects, either. But he was fascinated. For weeks, the scientist worked right through dinner. Then one day, he held a piece of lead between the tube and a piece of paper. The lead blocked the rays.

Something else amazed Roentgen. When he held up his hand, the shadow of his bones appeared on the paper. The rays passed through his flesh, but not through his bones. Roentgen tried it again and again to **confirm** the results.

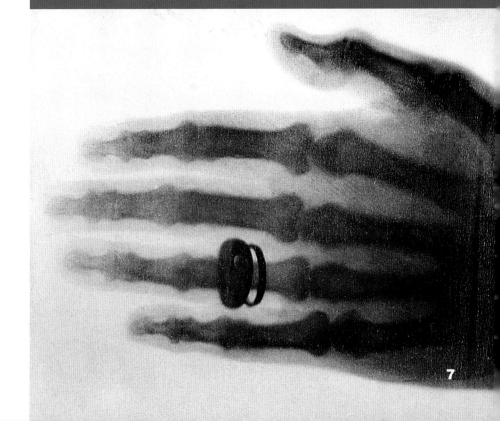

Bertha Roentgen's hand was one of the first X-rays ever made. When she saw her bones, she thought it was a sign that she was going to die soon.

This ray was a kind of **energy** no one had ever seen. In math, *X* is the symbol for the unknown. So, Roentgen named this ray an X-ray. Then he announced it to the world.

News of Roentgen's X-ray traveled fast. A French scientist named Henri Becquerel heard about this discovery. He had been studying **phosphorescent** rocks—rocks that glow in certain kinds of light. Maybe they were giving off X-rays, too.

Becquerel went back to his lab excited. He was working with a substance called **uranium**. He covered a photographic plate in black paper. He put the uranium on the plate. Then he left it.

When he came back, the uranium had made a gray smudge on the plate. The rays had passed right through the paper, like Roentgen's X-rays.

Where did the rays come from? There was no cathode ray tube. Becquerel had left the plate in the dark. So, the rays couldn't have been from the sun. There was no electrical current. The rays must have come from the uranium.

What made these strange and powerful rays? The answer lay inside the atom.

Inside the Atom

The idea of the atom is thousands of years old. A Greek philosopher named Democritus first came up with it. He lived about 2,400 years ago. He said that everything was made of tiny **particles**. At that time, the atom was just an idea. There were no experiments to prove that atoms existed.

For 2,300 years, atoms were thought to be the smallest things in the world. After Becquerel discovered uranium rays, scientists began to wonder. Maybe atoms were made of even smaller particles. If so, powerful forces, or bonds, must hold the parts of an atom together. What if some particles of an atom broke loose under certain conditions? The breaking of their bonds would release energy. Could these mysterious rays come from atoms breaking apart?

In 1896, Henri Becquerel discovered strange rays coming from the element uranium. Uranium is found in several minerals, including torbernite (shown at left).

9

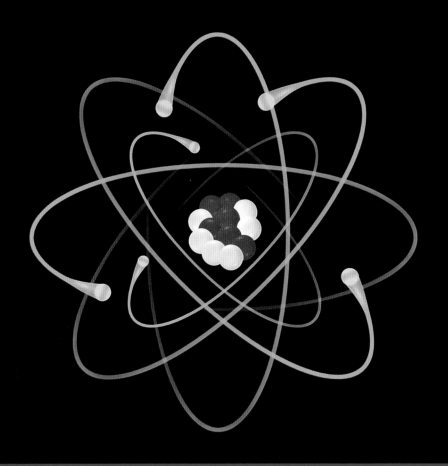

The nucleus of an atom looks a little like a bunch of grapes. It's made up of protons and neutrons. Electrons fly around the nucleus like a swarm of super-fast bugs.

The answer is yes. Over the next thirty years, scientists developed a model of the atom. It looked something like the diagram above. The center is called the **nucleus**. It has two kinds of particles in it: **neutrons** and **protons**. Other particles, called **electrons**, circle around the nucleus. They move incredibly fast. Under a very powerful microscope, they look like a gray cloud.

What keeps the electrons circling around the nucleus? Opposite magnetic charges keep them there. Electrons have a negative charge. Protons have a positive charge. The opposite charges attract each other. Neutrons are neither positive or negative. They are neutral.

Normally, things with a positive charge, like protons, repel each other. Then how do protons stay bunched up together in the nucleus? An incredibly powerful force in the nucleus holds the protons and neutrons together. It is called the strong force.

In most atoms, the particles stay perfectly in balance. Some atoms, though, are unstable. In these atoms, the nucleus can have too many or too few neutrons. What happens then? The atoms spit out particles to regain their balance. When the particles are released, the energy that held them may fly out in invisible waves. Together, the particles and the waves are called **radiation**.

Some elements, like uranium and radium, are particularly unstable. They are always seeking balance, and they are always releasing radiation. Today, scientists call elements like these **radioactive**. Roentgen and Becquerel were both studying radioactive substances. It was radiation that caused the strange events in both of their labs.

CHAPTER 2

The Amazing X-ray

X-rays made big headlines long before scientists could explain them. Newspapers everywhere printed Roentgen's photos. People were shocked and amazed. Some thought it was a trick. "There is no joke," a British paper reported. "It is a serious discovery by a serious German professor."

Some people were scared. Roentgen got one letter complaining that he had invented "death rays." Others worried that X-rays would allow people to see through clothes. One company actually sold "X-ray-proof" underwear.

Most people, though, were just fascinated. Photographers set up X-ray studios. Customers could buy a picture of their hand. Shoe stores used X-ray machines to make sure shoes fit perfectly. Thomas Edison, the great inventor, set up an X-ray machine in New York City. Thousands of people lined up for a look at their own skeletons. One person claimed he could X-ray people's heads to find out if they were criminals. A criminal skull, supposedly, looked different than a "normal" one.

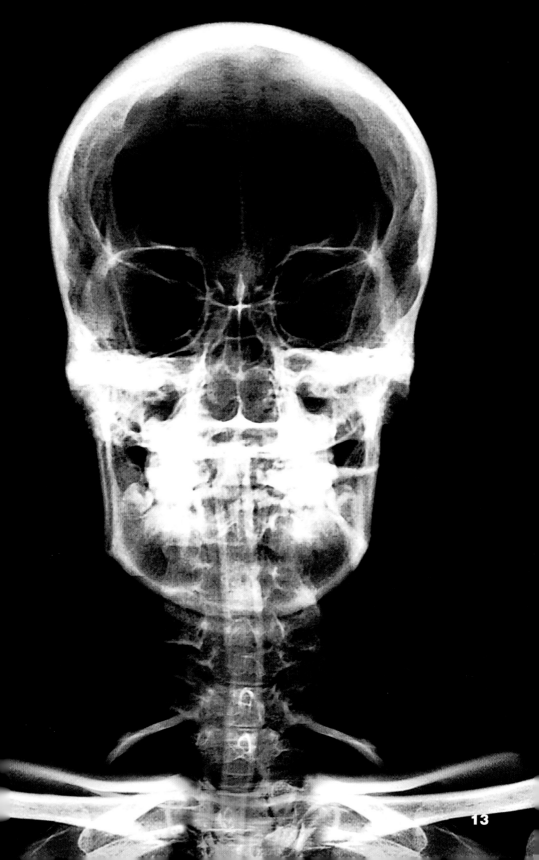

A Medical Miracle

One group of people knew right away that X-rays were serious business. Doctors quickly set up X-ray rooms and started experimenting. The results were exciting. Before X-rays, they could only guess what was happening inside a patient's body. Now, they could see if bones were broken. They could find bullets inside soldiers. One surgeon treated a young boy who had swallowed a belt buckle. X-rays **indicated** exactly where it was. The surgeon removed it safely.

Doctors soon discovered that the new rays could also be dangerous. Some tried a new procedure to remove scars or birthmarks with X-rays. Soon afterward, their patients lost big clumps of hair.

Scientists and doctors exposed their hands to the rays over and over. Their hands started to get sore. Red patches formed on their skin, just like a sunburn. Some doctors even had fingers and hands amputated. Thomas Edison's main assistant, Clarence Dally, worked for years with the rays. Consequently, he got serious burns. The burns turned into cancer. In 1904, he died after years of living in intense pain.

Safe Rays

Today, doctors have learned to use radiation safely. They protect patients with a lead blanket which blocks the rays. They use the lowest possible dose of rays. They take X-rays as quickly as possible.

Doctors have also come up with new ways to use radiation. Oddly enough, the same rays that caused Clarence Dally's cancer can also help treat it. Cancer is a disease in which cells grow fast and out of control. Radiation can kill cancer cells. It keeps the dangerous cells from taking over.

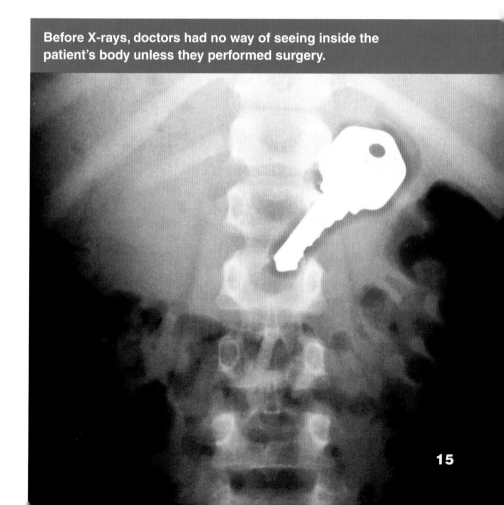

Before X-rays, doctors had no way of seeing inside the patient's body unless they performed surgery.

Radiation therapy must be done with care. X-rays can kill healthy cells as well as cancer cells. Doctors try to limit the damage. They find the exact location of tumors. Then, they focus the radiation only where the cancer cells are found.

Doctors still use X-rays to look through the skin. The images are more helpful than they were in Roentgen's time. Early X-ray pictures were cloudy and not very detailed. Today, computerized X-rays can show three-dimensional (3-D) images of the body. That's called a CT (or CAT) scan. This stands for Computed Axial Tomography. A CT scan fires low-level X-rays at a patient from all directions. The rays create detailed images of skulls, lungs, hearts, and other organs.

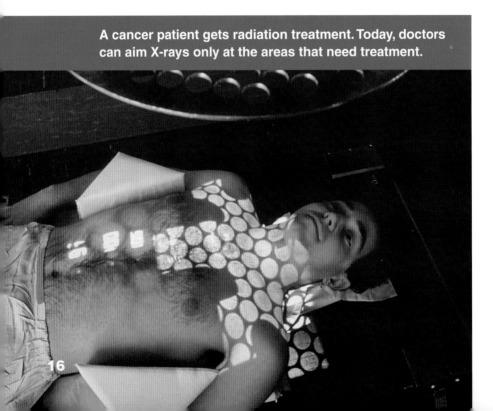

A cancer patient gets radiation treatment. Today, doctors can aim X-rays only at the areas that need treatment.

Surgeons use these scans to see the exact shape of tumors. They can find veins that might be blocked. This helps them treat diseases more effectively.

Radiation can even help doctors see inside your head. The process is called a PET scan. Doctors inject radioactive liquid into a patient's blood. The PET scan machine sees the radiation when the blood travels through the brain. When a part of the brain is active, it uses more blood. As a result, these active areas of the brain show up yellow or red on a computer screen.

PET scans have told scientists a lot about how the brain works. When we read, for instance, we use an area in the rear left part of the brain. It's called the visual cortex. When we listen to music, other parts of the brain light up on the PET scan.

Thanks to many new techniques, radiation helps millions of people recover from illnesses each year. We've come a long way since Roentgen first saw his hand bones. Who knows what the future of radioactive medicine holds?

THE Healer

One person, more than any other, taught the world how to heal people with radiation. Her name was Marie Curie.

In 1896, Marie was a graduate student living in France. Henri Becquerel had just discovered that uranium gave off mysterious rays. Marie was fascinated. She decided to look for other materials that produced the rays.

She and her husband, Pierre, spent their entire savings on their research. They worked in a cold, damp storeroom. They tested hundreds of materials.

Finally, they discovered radium. This element was incredibly powerful. It gave off heat. It glowed in the dark. Its rays were millions of times more powerful than uranium's rays. The Curies invented the term *radioactive* to describe it.

In 1903, Pierre and Marie Curie won the world's highest honor for their work. They were given the Nobel Prize in physics. That same year, Marie became the first woman in France to become a Doctor of Science.

Pierre died just three years later. Marie became even more devoted to her work. She started a research lab called the Radium Institute.

Before he died, Pierre had discovered that radium kills cancer cells. At the Institute, Marie developed ways to treat cancer patients with radium. The French called these treatments *Curietherapy* in honor of Marie.

In 1914, World War I interrupted the Institute's work. Marie joined the war effort. She organized a program to put X-ray machines on trucks. The trucks brought the machines to the battlefield. Marie and her teenage daughter Irene went along. They helped X-ray wounded soldiers. The X-rays helped doctors treat bullet wounds and broken bones.

In 1934, Marie died of a blood disease. The disease was probably caused by years of exposure to radiation. Marie's work had finally taken her life. Since then, it has saved countless others.

Marie Curie won the Nobel Prize twice for her work, once in 1903 and again in 1911.

CHAPTER 3

The Bomb

The year before Marie Curie died, a new idea was born. One day in 1933, a Hungarian scientist was walking through London. His name was Leo Szilard. By this time, scientists had figured out that radioactive atoms broke apart naturally. What would happen, Szilard wondered, if we tried to break an atom ourselves? It was an exciting idea. It was also terrifying. Splitting atoms could release huge amounts of energy. It could also make the world's most powerful bomb.

In 1942, that idea started to become a reality. World War II was raging all around the globe. The Japanese were fighting in the Pacific. German dictator Adolf Hitler had taken over much of Europe. Many European scientists fled to the United States. The government started a secret program called the Manhattan Project. European scientists teamed up with American scientists. Their job was to beat the Germans in a race to develop an atom-splitting bomb.

Led by **physicist** J. Robert Oppenheimer, the scientists went to work. The government built secret labs around the country. The scientists and their families moved in. They lived behind tall fences patrolled by guards. Security was tight. Everyone had to wear I.D. badges at all times. Government **censors** read all letters leaving the labs.

Inside the fences, the families had their own tiny cities. There were supermarkets and movie theaters. Babies were born. Kids went to school.

Meanwhile, in 1938, German scientists had split the uranium atom. They did it by shooting neutrons into the atom's nucleus. That caused the nucleus to split into pieces. As it split, the nucleus released neutrons, gamma rays, and other particles. The process was called **fission**.

Robert Oppenheimer (third from left) examines the site where a test bomb was exploded four weeks earlier.

Splitting one atom, however, didn't release enough energy. The scientists needed to split a lot of them at once. In late 1942, Oppenheimer's team figured out how. It happened in a secret experiment under the football field at the University of Chicago. Italian scientist Enrico Fermi built a device called a **nuclear reactor**. Inside it, he split uranium atoms. Those atoms released neutrons. The neutrons then split other atoms. More neutrons flew into the air. This led to still more split atoms. Finally, huge amounts of energy were released. Fermi had created the first nuclear **chain reaction**.

A neutron (shown in blue) hits a uranium atom. That atom splits into two smaller atoms and releases neutrons. Those neutrons split more uranium atoms. That's how a chain reaction works.

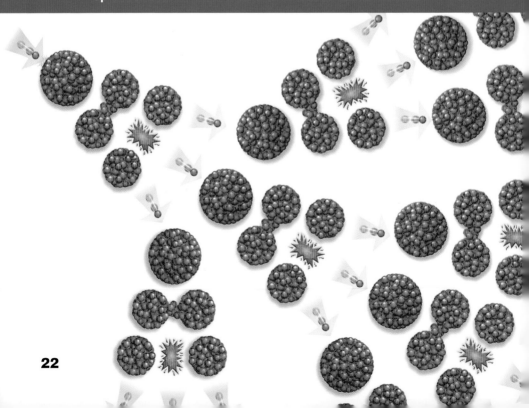

Now Oppenheimer wanted to know how to set off that chain reaction inside a bomb. The answer came at Los Alamos, New Mexico. Los Alamos was one of the secret labs in the Manhattan Project. The scientists there were working with two kinds of material, uranium and **plutonium**. They came up with two types of bombs, one using each material. They had to be very careful. If they calculated incorrectly, the bombs might never explode. Or worse, the bombs might explode during assembly.

Finally, one bomb was ready to test. The scientists picked an empty spot in the New Mexico desert. They built a 100-foot steel tower. They hung the bomb near the top.

On the morning of July 16, 1945, the scientists gathered at distant observation points. They stayed six to ten miles away from the bomb. No one knew what to expect. Some worried that the blast might set the air on fire. Others put on sun block to protect themselves from the rays.

Then, at 5:30 A.M., the bomb exploded. A blinding ball of fire leapt into the sky. Everyone watching was stunned. Scientist Philip Morrison felt like night had turned to day. "The thing that got me was ... the blinding heat of a bright day on your face in the cold desert morning," he said.

Now the United States controlled the terrible power of the bomb. By this time, the Germans had already surrendered. The Japanese, however, were still fighting. On August 6, 1945, an American bomber named the Enola Gay flew over Japan. It carried only a single weapon. It was a uranium bomb nicknamed "Little Boy." At 8:15 in the morning, Little Boy dropped from the plane. It exploded over the port city of Hiroshima.

The bomb's fireball was 100 meters (330 feet) across. Everything it touched immediately burned. Glass melted. Buildings crumbled from the shock.

Within seconds, most of the city was destroyed or on fire. Nearly 135,000 people were dead or badly injured. Three days later, a second bomb dropped. It fell on the city of Nagasaki. Finally, Japan surrendered. The war was over.

The atomic bomb deeply affected everyone on the Manhattan Project. Many, like Morrison, never worked with nuclear weapons again. Others, like Szilard, tried to stop countries from making them. Oppenheimer urged all nations to join together and fight the spread of nuclear weapons. He always remembered the sight of that first explosion. "We knew the world could not be the same," he said.

The first nuclear bomb hangs in its test tower. Soon, its power will change the world forever.

Energy from the Bomb

The Hiroshima bomb released a huge amount of energy. The energy traveled in waves from the explosion. As the waves traveled, they got weaker and weaker. (Throw a stone in a pond. Watch the ripples. You'll see the same effect.) Half of the bomb's energy came from the shock of the blast. It knocked down buildings 2 kilometers (1.24 miles) away. About 35 percent of the energy came from heat. It started fires all across the city. About 15 percent of the energy came from radiation.

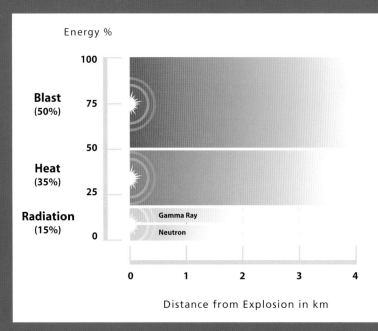

Atoms for Peace

Splitting an atom can produce the most dangerous explosion on Earth. It can also create something we all need: electricity. Thirty-one nations around the world have nuclear power plants. Those plants produce 16 percent of the world's electricity. They do it with fission. That's the same process that causes an atomic bomb to explode.

The difference is simple. In a bomb, the chain reaction is uncontrolled. Countless atoms split in a fraction of a second. The result is a huge blast. In a nuclear reactor, the reaction is controlled. It's slowed down to a safe level.

Here's how it works: When uranium atoms split, they release neutrons. Those neutrons split other atoms. The more neutrons released, the hotter and faster the reaction. In a nuclear power plant, control rods limit the amount of neutrons released. These rods are made of a special substance. They absorb neutrons so that fewer atoms split.

Putting the control rods into the reactor makes the reaction slow down. That causes the power level to drop. Pulling rods out makes the reaction speed up. Then the power increases. The diagram on the next page shows a nuclear power plant in action.

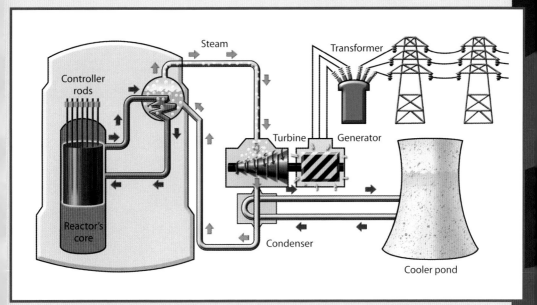

How a Nuclear Power Plant Works

1. Fission takes place in the reactor's core.

2. When the uranium atoms split, they give off heat.

3. Controller rods speed up or slow down the reaction.

4. The heat boils water into steam.

5. The steam travels like wind through a pipe. It turns a wheel of big blades called a turbine.

6. The turning blades have mechanical energy. That energy is turned into electricity in a machine called a **generator**. The electricity flows out of the plant in wires and ends up in your home.

7. Meanwhile, a condenser cools the steam. That turns it back into water. The water is then pumped back into the core to make more steam.

8. The nuclear power plant has many safety features to prevent a **meltdown**. A meltdown is when the reactor's core overheats and melts. That would release harmful radiation into the air.

Glossary

atom (*noun*) the smallest part of an element that has all the properties of that element

bond (*noun*) a connection that ties or holds things together

censor (*noun*) a person who looks at movies, books, or mail to take out harmful material

chain reaction (*noun*) a series of events in which one thing causes the next, as in a line of falling dominoes

confirm (*verb*) to prove something true or correct

electron (*noun*) a tiny particle found in the nucleus of an atom. It has a negative electrical charge

element (*noun*) one of the basic parts of matter; a substance that cannot be split into a simpler substance

energy (*noun*) the power or ability to do work

fission (*noun*) a nuclear reaction in which an atom is split apart to produce energy or an explosion

generator (*noun*) a machine that uses mechanical energy to make electricity

indicate (*verb*) to show or signal something

meltdown (*noun*) the overheating of a nuclear reactor's core

nuclear reactor (*noun*) a device used to split atoms

nucleus (*noun*) the center of an atom. It contains protons and neutrons

neutron (*noun*) a tiny particle in the nucleus of an atom. It has no electrical charge

particle (*noun*) an extremely small piece of something

phosphorescent (*adjective*) giving off light without an energy source

physicist (*noun*) a scientist who studies matter, energy, space, and time

plutonium (*noun*) a highly radioactive substance made from uranium

proton (*noun*) a tiny particle in the nucleus of an atom. It has a positive electrical charge

radiation (*noun*) energy particles that travel in waves out from a radioactive substance

radioactive (*adjective*) the giving off of energy after atoms split apart

uranium (*noun*) a radioactive element that is used as a source of nuclear energy

Idioms

the thing that got me (*page 23*) what was surprising or unusual

The thing that got me about the movie was the music.

Index